KINGFISHER DIPPERS

Jungle Animals

Jenny Wood

Kingfisher Books

Kingfisher Books, Grisewood & Dempsey Ltd,
Elsley House, 24–30 Great Titchfield Street,
London W1P 7AD.

First published in 1990 by Kingfisher Books

BRITISH LIBRARY CATALOGUING IN PUBLICATION DATA
Wood, Jenny
    Jungle animals.
    1. Jungles. Vertebrates
    I. Title II. Robson, Eric III. Series
    596.0909'52
ISBN 0-86272-507-0

Edited by Mike Halson
Designed by Ben White
Cover design by David Jefferis
Illustrated by Hayward Art Group; Eric Robson/*Garden Studio*;
    Peter Stephenson/*Jillian Burgess*

Phototypeset by Southern Positives and Negatives (SPAN),
Lingfield, Surrey
Printed in Spain

Contents

Deep in the Jungle   4

Layers of Life   6

A Miniature Jungle   8

Jungle Birds   10

Jungle Cats   12

Animals in Danger   14

Jungle Activities   16

Monkeys and Apes   18

Life in the Water   20

Small Jungle Dwellers   22

Night-time Animals   24

Animal Disguises   26

Jungle File   28

Glossary   30

Index   32

If you find an unusual or difficult word in this book, check for an explanation in the glossary on pages 30 and 31.

Deep in the Jungle

The air is so hot and damp that you can hardly breathe. Your shirt sticks to your back as you push your way through the undergrowth. Weak rays of sunlight peep through the giant trees which tower above you, creating patches of light and shade on the forest floor. Dead leaves and fallen branches are everywhere. A small animal suddenly appears in front of you, then scurries out of sight. In the distance, a jaguar snarls. Overhead, monkeys howl and birds screech. This is the jungle.

All the jungle animals shown here live in South America. On other pages, labels near the animals tell you which area they come from. The jungle map on pages 28–29 shows where that area is.

Layers of Life

The world's biggest jungles lie either side of the Equator. They are known as rainforests because of their high rainfall. The rainforests are packed with all kinds of vegetation, from giant trees to creepers, shrubs and small plants. All this greenery divides up into four different layers – like a sandwich.

In the rainforest only a few animals live on the ground. Most are to be found up in the mass of leaves and branches called the canopy, where there is a constant supply of things to eat.

Emergent layer
The tallest trees grow up to around 55 metres, to get more sunlight. Some grow special roots down from their branches for extra support.

Canopy layer
Trees here grow to a height of 30 metres. Most of their leaves and branches are right at the top of the trunk and form a thick, shady roof.

Middle layer
This layer is formed by smaller trees about 15 metres high, with spindly trunks. They grow wherever light pierces down from the canopy.

Shrub layer
Plants cannot grow without light, and so the gloomy floor of the jungle has only a few shrubs, ferns and fungi among the dead leaves and branches.

7

A Miniature Jungle

The hot, damp climate of a jungle is ideal for plants to grow. You can create the same conditions in a miniature jungle of your own. To do this, you need to make a miniature greenhouse which keeps the plants warm and damp. It will last for months, so find a good place to keep it before you start.

HOW A JUNGLE WORKS
In jungle areas the Sun is at its strongest, but there is also very high rainfall. The thick canopy formed by tree branches and leaves helps seal in the heat and dampness, making the jungle a hot and sticky place where plants can grow all year long.

1: Here is what you need to make your jungle: potting compost; a seed tray with holes in the bottom; sand; a tray larger than your seed tray; a watering can; a spoon; a plastic fish tank large enough to fit over the seed tray; and some small pot plants such as ferns, African violets and begonias.

2: Three-quarters fill the seed tray with potting compost. Now half-fill the large tray with sand and pat it down smoothly. Dampen the sand using the watering can. Place the seed tray in the middle of the sand. The damp sand will keep your miniature jungle constantly moist – just like the real thing.

3: Use the spoon to dig a hole where the first plant is to go. Then take the first pot and hold it with the fingers of one hand over the soil. Turn the pot upside down and gently remove the plant and soil. Put the plant in the hole and fill in the gaps with extra compost. Plant the rest in the same way.

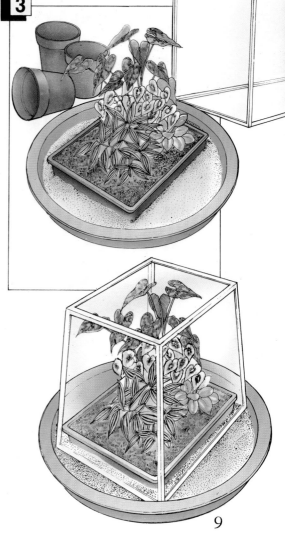

▶ Place the fish tank carefully over the plants. Keep your miniature jungle in a light place but not in strong sunlight. The plants will grow well, provided you always keep the sand damp. After a few months your plants will have grown quite big. Use a pair of scissors to clip them back into shape.

9

Jungle Birds

More kinds of birds live in the jungle than in any other place. Most are to be found high up amongst the branches of the canopy, where they can feed on the plentiful flowers, fruit and nuts. Some birds soar high above, swooping down from time to time to snatch up other birds, bats and even monkeys.

Many jungle birds are spectacularly coloured, making them easy to see against the green canopy.

Greater bird of paradise
Papua New Guinea

Scarlet macaw
Central and South
America

Hummingbird
North, Central
and South America

Jungle birds feed in lots of
different ways. Toucans use
their large beaks to tear off
chunks of fruit, while parrots
use their powerful bills to crack
nuts. Tiny hummingbirds, on
the other hand, daintily sip
nectar from treetop flowers as
they hover in mid-air.

Black cockatoo
Australia and
Papua New Guinea

African grey parrot
Africa

Toco toucan
South America

Jungle Cats

The fiercest hunters in the jungle are the big cats.
With their great agility and speed they are able to
track down and kill almost any other animal. All of
them have patterns of spots or stripes on their coats
to make them hard to see in the patchy sunlight
below the jungle canopy. Many of them are good
climbers, using their tails for balance and their
strong claws to grip the branches.

▼ The leopard comes from
Africa and Southern Asia. It
often sleeps lying along a
branch and usually drags its
kill up into a tree to eat, away
from other thieving animals.

▼ The jaguar is found in North,
Central and South America. As
well as being a good climber, it
is a strong swimmer and often
eats fish and other creatures
from the river.

◄ The Bengal tiger lives in the grassy jungles of India and its neighbouring countries. It hunts alone, slowly and carefully stalking its prey under cover of the long grass.

► The tiger creeps up as near as it can to its prey. It crouches down like an ordinary cat, waiting for the right moment to leap out and make a surprise attack.

◄ In a blur of speed, the tiger leaps out from its cover. Its startled victim has almost no time to make an escape, and the attack is over in seconds.

The tiger is truly Lord of the Jungle. It is the largest and strongest member of the cat family, with males nearly three metres long from their nose to the tip of their tail. Its speed of attack makes it the most fearsome of all hunters.

Animals in Danger

Many of the animals in this book, including tigers, gorillas and orang-utans, are fast dying out. Their main enemy is not other animals, but people. Hunting, pollution and the cutting down of jungles have wiped out over 60 types of mammals and birds in the past 50 years. Efforts are now being made to help save all animals in danger – but for many it may already be too late.

▲ The rhinoceros is one of the world's fastest disappearing animals. The rarest type is the Javan rhino, shown here.

Although rhinos are best known for their pointed horns, Javans often have little or no horn at all.

▲ The aye-aye lemur comes from Madagascar, off the east coast of Africa. It feeds by pulling insects out of their holes with its long third finger. Sadly, this strange animal is now almost extinct.

▲ Like its relative the rhinoceros, the tapir has changed little since the age of the dinosaurs. This odd-looking animal was once widespread, but it is now only found in a few remote areas of the world.

▲ The monkey-eating eagle is a native of the Philippine Islands in Asia. The destruction of its forest home has reduced its numbers to about 100. A last-minute campaign has now been started to try to stop it disappearing for ever.

Jungle Activities

To make a simple jungle kite, you will need: a large rectangle of paper; a light garden cane; a stapler; a sharpened pencil; sticky tape; and a reel of cotton.

1: Fold the paper in half as shown.

2: Fold back equal parts of each half to make a kite shape.

3: Turn the kite over and staple it together. Use the pencil to make some small holes along the spine of the kite.

4: Use sticky tape to tape over the gap down the front of the kite. Tape the cane across the front to hold the flaps in place. Thread a piece of cotton through a hole near the top of the kite's spine and the rest of the reel through a hole near the bottom. Tie the two pieces together as shown below. You may need to try different holes to make the kite fly better.

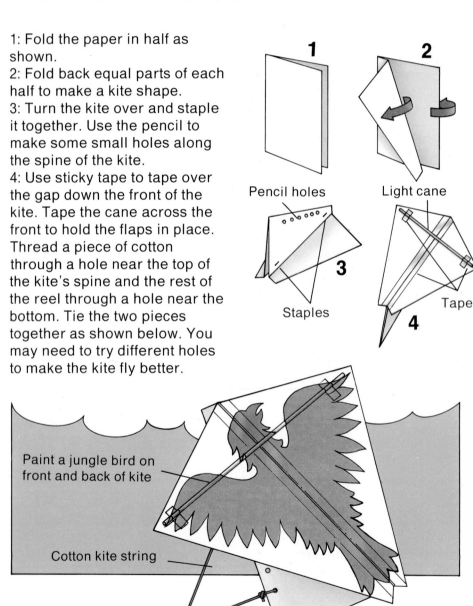

Pencil holes

Light cane

Staples

Tape

Paint a jungle bird on front and back of kite

Cotton kite string

16

ANIMAL MASKS

Animal masks are easy to make and great fun to wear. All you need for a home-made mask is: a plain paper plate; some elastic; scissors. Decorate the mask with paint or felt pens, and glue on feathers, wool or card.

1: Draw an animal face on the paper plate. Ask an adult to cut out the eye holes and two small holes for the elastic.

2: Thread the elastic through the holes to hold the mask on.

3: Add extra decoration to finish off the mask. Why not make lots of different masks for your friends?

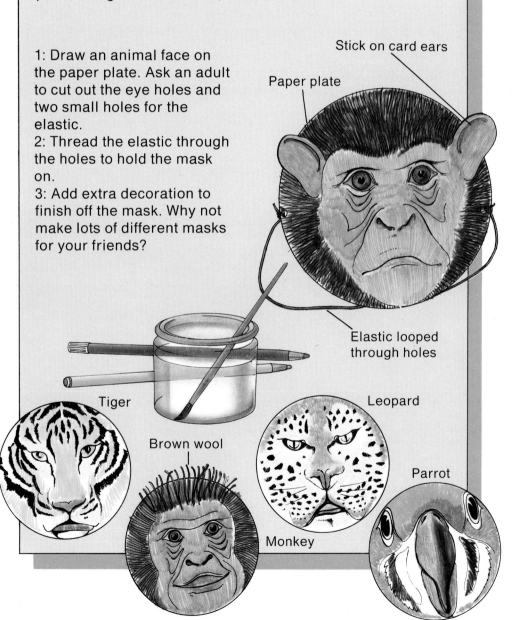

Stick on card ears

Paper plate

Elastic looped through holes

Tiger

Brown wool

Leopard

Parrot

Monkey

Monkeys and Apes

Monkeys and apes are among the noisiest and liveliest of the jungle creatures. They usually live up in the canopy and are excellent climbers, swinging and leaping with ease from branch to branch.

Most monkeys, like those shown below, have a tail. They use it for balance or to help grip branches. Apes do not have tails. There are only four types: three are shown on the opposite page and the other, the chimpanzee, can be seen on page 2.

Colobus monkey
Africa

Entellus langur
Asia

Black spider monkey
South America

Gibbon
Asia

Orang-utan
Asia

The menacing-looking gorilla from Africa is actually a very gentle, peace-loving animal. Gorillas live in families, and spend most of the day on the ground eating fruit, roots, bark and leaves. At night, they make beds of twigs in low tree branches.

19

Life in the Water

Tropical jungles are the rainiest places in the world. Much of the rainfall either collects on the ground in swamps or lakes, or flows in rivers back into the oceans. And wherever there is water there is a massive variety of

Tropical rivers can be dangerous places to swim in. If you are not squeezed to death by an anaconda or crunched by a caiman, you could still be eaten alive by a shoal of deadly piranha fish!

Capybara

Lungfish

Angel fish

Discus fish

wildlife – insects, fish, reptiles and mammals.

The scene below shows a view of life above and below the water in the South American Amazonian rainforest. There are creatures of all shapes and sizes, from tiny insects to giant snakes and strange land-dwellers such as the capybara, a kind of giant guinea pig.

Anaconda

The Amazon River contains around 2000 types of fish, many of which are very beautiful. They are a common sight in tropical fish tanks.

Caiman

Piranha fish

Electric eel

Small Jungle Dwellers

On the jungle floor there is little light and few plants can survive. The ground is covered with dead leaves and fallen branches which rot very quickly in the moist heat. This provides little food for larger animals, but is an ideal diet for smaller creatures such as insects and worms. There are also all kinds of spiders which prey on insects and sometimes birds and other small animals too.

Leafcutter ants slice up leaves with their powerful jaws and carry them away. The Goliath beetle is the heaviest insect in the world. Leeches are worms that feed by sucking blood.

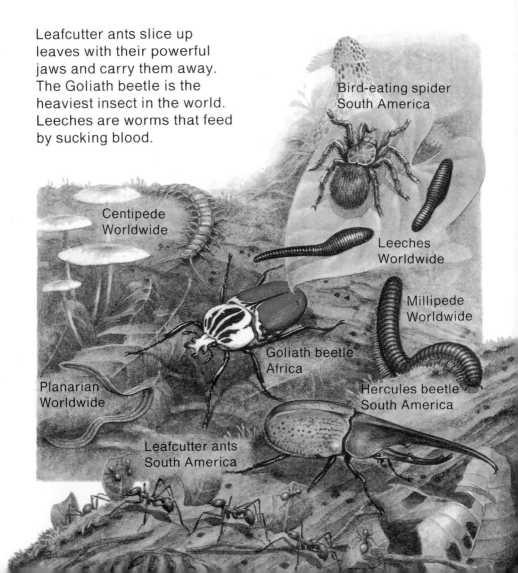

Bird-eating spider
South America

Centipede
Worldwide

Leeches
Worldwide

Millipede
Worldwide

Goliath beetle
Africa

Hercules beetle
South America

Planarian
Worldwide

Leafcutter ants
South America

Tropical jungles have frequent rainfall and no changes of season. There are huge numbers of plants in flower at all times. These are ideal conditions for butterflies and moths – and the jungles are full of them. They come in all shapes and sizes, and an amazing range of beautiful patterns and dazzling colours.

Milionia paradisea
Papua New Guinea

Small postman
South America

Emperor moth
Africa

Morpho cypris
South America

Cotton wool pad

Birdwing
Asia and New Guinea

Attract butterflies into your garden using a plate with a cotton wool pad in the middle. Fill the plate with nectar made from half a teaspoon of honey, half a teaspoon of sugar and two cups of water.

23

Night-time Animals

The jungle is a busy place at night as well as during the day. There are many animals which can find their way around perfectly well in the deep gloom below the canopy. To do this they use a variety of highly developed senses. Some have huge eyes to see better, and others have a good sense of smell. Snakes such as the bushmaster hunt by detecting the heat given out from the bodies of their prey.

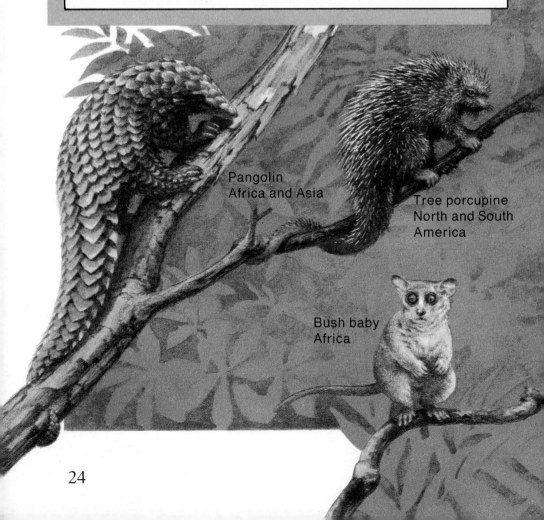

Pangolin
Africa and Asia

Tree porcupine
North and South
America

Bush baby
Africa

Vampire bat
Central and South
America

Bats use sound to work out
where they are going.
They give out high-pitched
squeaks and identify
shapes from the way the
sounds echo back to them.
The vampire bats shown
here feed by sucking their
victims' blood while they
are sleeping.

Tarsier
Asia

Slender loris
Asia

Nine-banded armadillo
North, South and
Central America

Bushmaster
Central and South America

Moon rat
Asia

Animal Disguises

Most jungle animals are the prey of other animals. One way of avoiding being an easy meal is to make yourself more difficult to see. Because of this, the jungle is full of animals trying to look as if they are part of the scenery. Using disguise in this way is called camouflage. Unfortunately for these animals, their enemies, or predators, sometimes use the same trick, allowing them to sneak up close to their victims without being seen.

▲ The chameleon is an African lizard which changes the colour of its skin to match its surroundings or its mood. It moves very slowly, which is another way to avoid attracting the attention of a predator.

▲ The dangerous Gaboon viper also comes from Africa. It is perfectly camouflaged for moving through the dead leaves on the jungle floor.

▲ Stick insects are found in many areas. They manage to look just like twigs and are almost impossible to see. Some types have flattened green bodies and look like leaves instead.

▲ The slow-moving three-toed sloth is from South America. It spends most of its time hanging upside down from trees, looking like an ants' nest or a mass of leaves. Its hair is often covered with green slime.

Jungle File

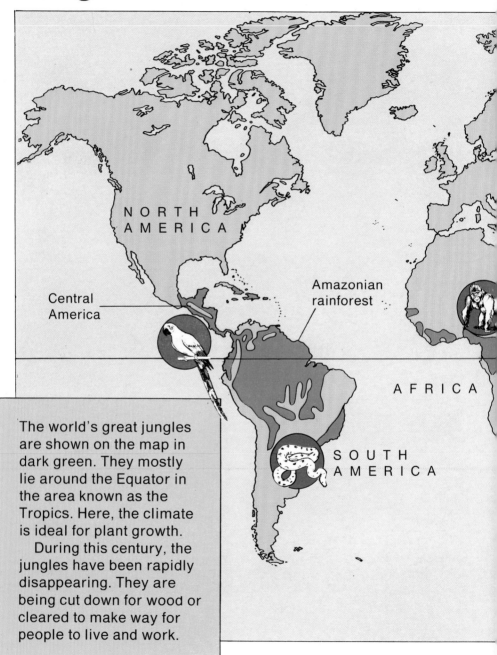

NORTH AMERICA

Central America

Amazonian rainforest

AFRICA

SOUTH AMERICA

The world's great jungles are shown on the map in dark green. They mostly lie around the Equator in the area known as the Tropics. Here, the climate is ideal for plant growth.

During this century, the jungles have been rapidly disappearing. They are being cut down for wood or cleared to make way for people to live and work.

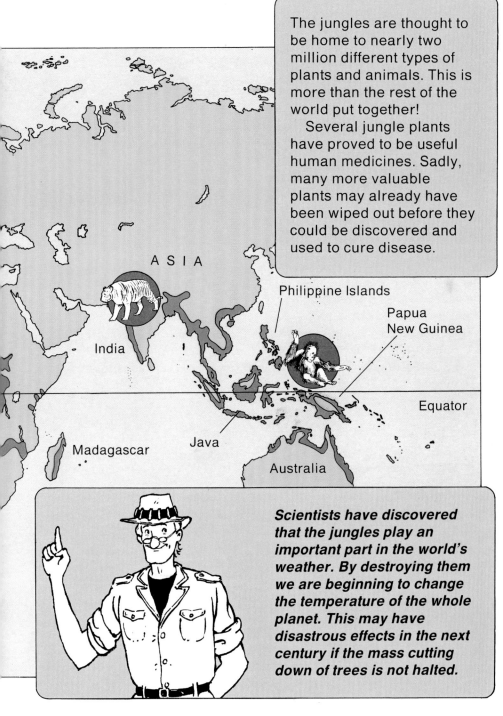

The jungles are thought to be home to nearly two million different types of plants and animals. This is more than the rest of the world put together!

Several jungle plants have proved to be useful human medicines. Sadly, many more valuable plants may already have been wiped out before they could be discovered and used to cure disease.

ASIA

Philippine Islands

Papua
New Guinea

India

Equator

Madagascar

Java

Australia

Scientists have discovered that the jungles play an important part in the world's weather. By destroying them we are beginning to change the temperature of the whole planet. This may have disastrous effects in the next century if the mass cutting down of trees is not halted.

Glossary

Amazonian rainforest
The rainforest in South America through which the River Amazon flows. It is by far the largest rainforest, covering about one-third of the continent.

Big cats
The larger members of an animal family that includes the household cat. They all have agile bodies, strong teeth and sharp claws. As well as tigers, leopards and jaguars, the best-known big cats are lions. These live in open grasslands rather than in jungles.

Climate
The usual weather of one area. The climate in a jungle is hot and wet, while the climate in the Arctic is cold and snowy.

Creepers
Plants that grow up other plants. Huge, thick creepers such as lianas are used by monkeys and apes as they swing from tree to tree.

Equator
An imaginary line around the centre of the Earth, halfway between the North Pole and the South Pole. At the Equator, the Sun is extremely hot, and the weather is warm all year round.

Extinct
This word is used when a type of animal or plant has died out altogether. An example of this is the dinosaurs, which became extinct millions of years ago.

Fungi
Mushrooms and toadstools are fungi. They have no leaves, flowers or green colouring, and grow where it is dark and damp.

Hunting
A large number of animals are hunted by people for their meat, skins, horns or tusks. This has greatly reduced their numbers and hunting is now banned by many countries.

Jungle
An area of thick forest found in hot countries. Jungles near the Equator are also known as rainforests because of their heavy rainfall. Not all jungles are filled with trees – the Indian jungle, for example, is made up of thick grass and bushes instead.

Lizard
A four-legged reptile with a long tail. They are often hard to see – such as the iguana on the bottom right of page 5.

Mammals
Warm-blooded animals which feed their young with milk from the mother's body. They are the most intelligent type of animals, especially monkeys, apes and humans.

Pollution
The spoiling of air, water and land by poisonous waste. Pollution damages plant life and is a constant danger to animals.

Predator
An animal that hunts other animals for food.

Prey
An animal that is hunted by another animal. Most animals are prey to other animals; only a few, such as the tiger, have no predators at all.

Reptile
A cold-blooded animal with a dry, scaly skin. Caimans, snakes and lizards are all reptiles.

Shrub
A large bushy plant.

Swamp
An area of wet, spongy ground. Swamps are common around the outer edges of jungles.

Tropical jungle
A jungle which lies in the area of the Tropics.

Tropics
The region either side of the Equator where the weather is very hot.

Undergrowth
Small trees, shrubs and other plants growing beneath other vegetation.

Index

African grey parrot 11
anaconda 20, 21
angel fish 20
aye-aye lemur 15

bird-eating spider 22
black cockatoo 11
black spider monkey 18
bush baby 24
bushmaster snake 24, 25
butterflies 23

caiman 20, 21, 31
capybara 20, 21
chameleon 26
chimpanzee 18
colobus monkey 18

discus fish 20

electric eel 21
entellus langur 18

Gaboon viper 27
gibbon 19
Goliath beetle 22
gorilla 14, 19
greater bird of paradise 10

Hercules beetle 22
hummingbird 10, 11

iguana 31

jaguar 4, 12, 20, 30
Javan rhino 14

leafcutter ants 22
leeches 22
leopard 12, 17, 30
lizard 26, 31
lungfish 20

millipede 22
monkey-eating eagle 15
moon rat 25
moths 23

nine-banded armadillo 25

orang-utan 14, 19

pangolin 24
piranha fish 20, 21

rhinoceros 14, 15

scarlet macaw 10
slender loris 25
stick insects 27

tapir 15
tarsier 25
three-toed sloth 27
tiger 13, 14, 17, 30
toco toucan 11
tree porcupine 24

vampire bat 25